THE
IMMUNE SYSTEM
YOUR MAGIC
DOCTOR

❊ ❊ ❊ ❊ ❊

A GUIDE TO THE IMMUNE SYSTEM
FOR THE CURIOUS OF ALL AGES

by
Helen Garvy

illustrated by
Dan Bessie

Shire Press 26873 Hester Creek Road, Los Gatos, CA 95030

Based on an award-winning film by Helen Garvy and Dan Bessie
(Distributed by Barr Films, P.O. Box 7878, Irwindale, CA, 91706-7878)

Medical consultant: Henry Hilgard, M.D., Professor of Immunology,
University of California, Santa Cruz

Illustration coloring by Karen Gibbs.

Typography by Dickie Magidoff, Archetype Typography, Berkeley

Special thanks also to Brigid McCaw, M.D.; Alan Steinbach, M.D.;
Oliver Fein, M.D.; and Carolyn Craven.

Library of Congress Catalogue Card Number: 91-091575

ISBN: 0-918828-09-0 (hardback)
ISBN: 0-918828-10-4 (paperback)

SHIRE PRESS
26873 Hester Creek Road
Los Gatos, CA 95030
(408) 353-4253

Contents

✿ ✿ ✿ ✿ ✿

BUY MY
POSIES TO
CURE YE
POX

Your Magic Doctor

For a very long time, thousands and thousands of years in fact, people didn't really know very much about how or why they got sick. Some of our ancestors had ideas about how our bodies worked and they discovered some natural remedies to treat diseases. But too often they relied on magic and superstition and guesswork—and most of the cures they tried were completely useless.

1

Today we've learned a lot about how the body works and about health and disease—and doctors can help cure many illnesses. But did you know that your own body usually can and does take care of most things that go wrong all by itself?

That's right! Your body has its very own built-in 'magic doctor'—the immune system—that helps keep you well and helps heal you when you get sick. Let's look at how it all works.

Outside Defenses: The Fortress

You might think of your body as kind of a fortress. And, of course, as with a fortress, there are always lots of things trying to get in—a whole invading army of **microorganisms**—**bacteria, viruses,** and **fungi,**—and the chemical and other poisons that exist all around in the environment.

These tiny microorganisms—
commonly called **germs**—can
cause disease and infection. But
your body has many ways to fight
back against the invaders and there
is a constant battle between the
invading germs and your body's
outer and inner defenses.

*Boldface words are in the glossary.

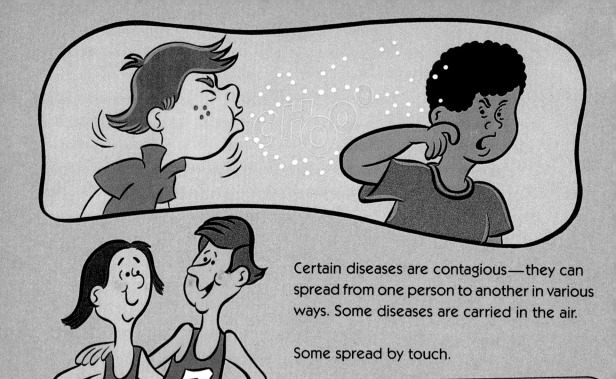

Certain diseases are contagious—they can spread from one person to another in various ways. Some diseases are carried in the air.

Some spread by touch.

Other diseases are carried by blood or other body fluids and those fluids need to come in contact with one another to spread the disease. Still other diseases, such as cancer, are not contagious but develop inside our bodies.

On the outside you're protected from many of the invaders that cause disease by your skin, which doesn't let most of them even get past the surface.

Washing regularly gets rid of millions of germs.

7

Airborne germs, which try to enter through one of the openings in the body, also have a tough time.

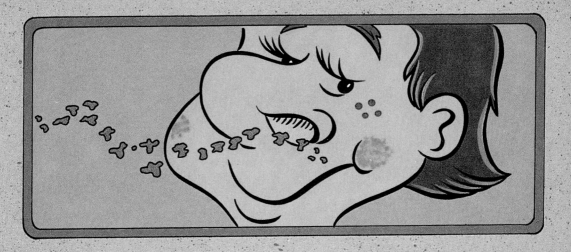

Your nose, for instance, has tiny hairs inside which serve as guards to keep out invaders. Your eyelashes and eyelids keep away more germs. And the nose and mouth both have mucus to trap invaders—kind of like the moat around a fortress.

Sometimes, when enemies do manage to get inside, your body instinctively tries to get rid of them. You sneeze, or vomit, or your eyes fill with tears.

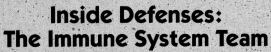

Inside Defenses:
The Immune System Team

But what happens when an invader does succeed in slipping completely past this first line of defense?

That's where your 'magic doctor'—the **immune system**—comes in. The immune system's main defending army consists of your **white blood cells** —and there are millions of them.

If you look at your blood under a microscope, you'll be able to see these white blood cells which help fight disease.

RED CELLS

WHITE CELLS

PLASMA

PLATELETS

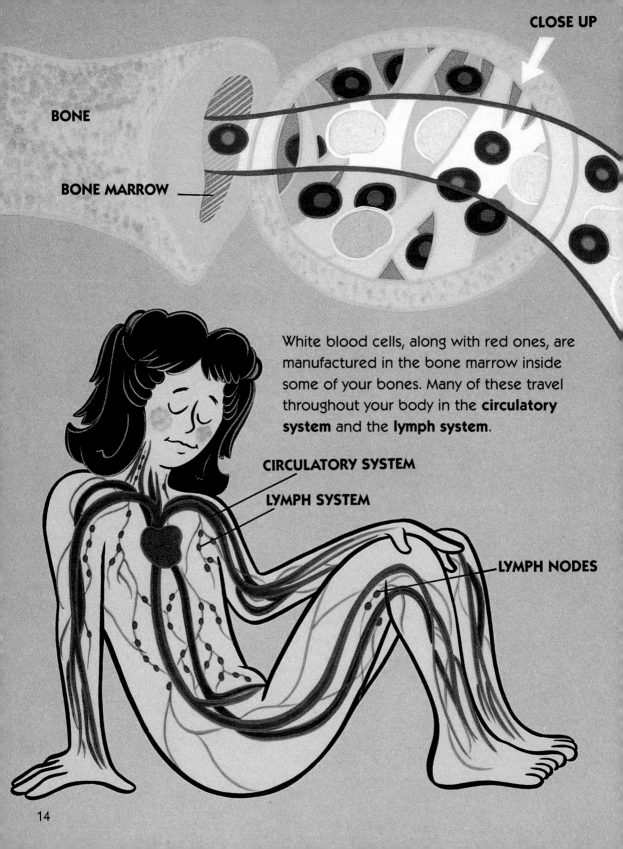

CLOSE UP

BONE

BONE MARROW

White blood cells, along with red ones, are manufactured in the bone marrow inside some of your bones. Many of these travel throughout your body in the **circulatory system** and the **lymph system**.

CIRCULATORY SYSTEM

LYMPH SYSTEM

LYMPH NODES

14

But let's go back to the white cells. There are several different kinds of white cells—each with its own special job and its own name. Let's meet some of the most important ones.

White cells called **phagocytes** (which means 'cell-eaters') engulf and destroy invading bacteria and other unwanted cells. **Macrophages** and **Neutrophils** are the two main kinds of phagocytes.

MACROPHAGE   **NEUTROPHIL**

Other white blood cells called **lymphocytes** become B or T cells. The future **B cells** travel directly to the lymph nodes located in various parts of the body where they wait until they are called on to make **antibodies**.

TO THE LYMPH NODES

THYMUS

The future **T cells** travel to a gland located near the heart, called the **thymus**—

16

where they sort of 'go to school' to learn how to become special kinds of T cells—**Helper T cells, Killer T cells,** and **Suppressor T cells**.

All the different kinds of white cells work together—and keep in touch through a marvelous communication network. They're all part of your 'magic doctor' and their main job is to identify and destroy any invader that doesn't belong in your body and could make you sick.

How the Immune System Works

Now let's take a closer look at what happens when invading bacteria or viruses get by the outside defenses—and your immune system, the army of white blood cells we've just met, swings into action.

The first white blood cells an invader might meet are the roving sentries called Neutrophils, followed soon by the Macrophages.

GARBAGE

Some invaders, such as most bacteria for example, are simply destroyed on the spot by these powerful white cells.

Under a microscope, we could actually watch a Macrophage engulf and then eat an invader, turning it into harmless pieces.

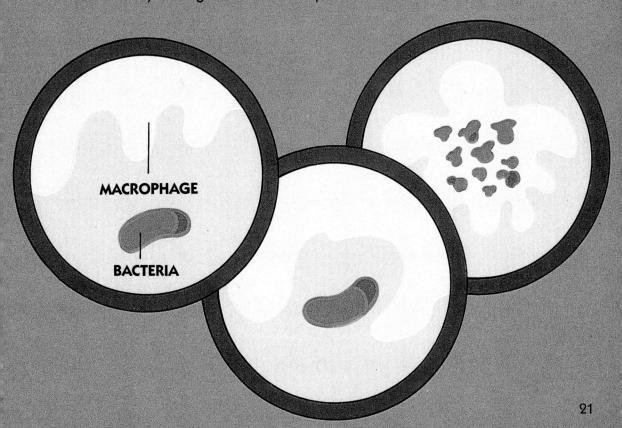

MACROPHAGE

BACTERIA

This is routine work for these white cells. They are scavengers and are constantly destroying all kinds of outside invaders and cleaning up inside the body. We just never notice when they do their job well.

Some invaders, certain bacteria for example, are so powerful, or there are so many of them, that the Neutrophils and Macrophages need extra help.

When these sentries recognize that the enemies are too strong for them to handle they immediately call for reinforcements from the rest of the immune system.

The white blood cells called Helper T cells are the first to respond.

Their first step is to identify the enemy—and they work like detectives. Each invader is recognized by its special code or mark—kind of like a fingerprint—which will aid in its identification. These markings are called **antigens**.

ANTIGEN

ANTIBODY WORKSHOP

As soon as they know exactly who the enemy is, the Helper T cells call for more help—from the special white blood cells called B cells, who have set up shop in the lymph nodes. Certain B cells immediately begin reproducing themselves and producing antibodies, special substances which match the antigen of that particular invader.

The antibodies attach themselves to the antigens of the invaders.

Once the invaders are marked or neutralized by the antibodies, other white cells, including the Macrophages, come in to destroy them.

GARBAGE

With a microscope we can see it all happen. Antibodies hook up with the antigens on the invading bacteria, making them defenseless and vulnerable to the Macrophages who rush in to finish the job.

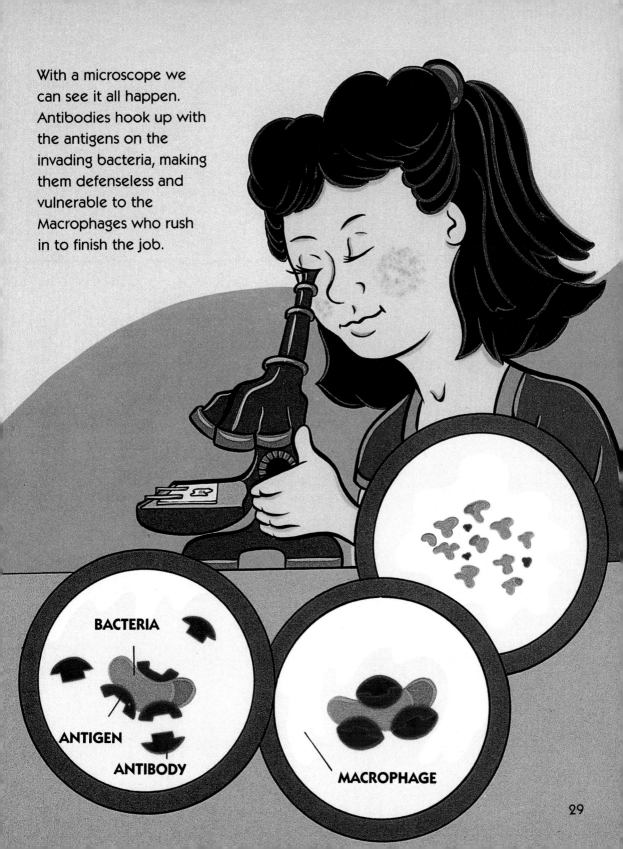

BACTERIA

ANTIGEN

ANTIBODY

MACROPHAGE

Viruses, such as those that cause colds for instance, are sneakier than bacteria and harder to get rid of. They are often smaller and more numerous than bacteria and they work in different ways.

Viruses actually hide in regular cells in the body—

where the viruses then grow and multiply

and finally burst out of the host cell, releasing thousands of new viruses.

Each new virus takes over another cell—and the cycle begins again.

When this happens, the sentries call in reinforcements —the Killer T cells!

32

The Killer T cells kill the host cell—the cell which was taken over—and the invading virus dies along with it.

If any of the viruses escape, antibodies lock on to them, trapping them until the Macrophages arrive to eat them up.

When the defenders have won and the invaders have been defeated, another part of the immune system team, the Suppressor T cells, step in to bring an end to the fighting—and everything goes back to normal.

Except that special **Memory T cells** and **Memory B cells** stick around to remember that particular invader's fingerprints—or antigens.

Then if another invader of the same kind ever returns, the team will be ready and able to fight back much more quickly, with less time wasted and less damage done to other cells. Because of this, there are many diseases, such as measles, that you can only get once. This is what we call **immunity**—the ability to resist a particular disease.

Although your magic doctor responds differently to each particular invader, those are the main members of the defending army—Macrophages, Neutrophils, B cells, Helper T cells, Killer T cells, Suppressor T cells, Memory T cells, and Memory B cells.

What Can Go Wrong

As amazing as the immune system is, sometimes it doesn't work as it should.

Sometimes the immune system makes a mistake and attacks harmless visitors, such as pollen from plants, and we develop symptoms such as sneezing, itching, rashes, or a runny nose.

We call these reactions **allergies**.

Sometimes, but not very often, the system makes a mistake and attacks normal cells, thinking they are outside invaders. This is what happens in **autoimmune** diseases, such as rheumatoid arthritis or multiple sclerosis, where the immune system attacks certain parts of the body.

Sometimes one or more parts of the immune system are missing or defective.

Some children, whom we call **immunodeficient**, are born without natural inner defenses and need special protection against bacteria and viruses. Since their bodies can't fight off even simple diseases, they can get very sick and even die from minor illnesses.

Sometimes when just a part of the immune system is affected, it can cripple the whole team. This is what happens when the **AIDS** virus destroys the Helper T cells which would normally call in reinforcements. That's why people with AIDS have trouble fighting off invaders.

Sometimes we get sick because the immune system fails to recognize invaders. There are so many kinds of cold and flu viruses that the sentries have a hard time recognizing them, and the viruses can become well established before they are finally discovered.

Cancer begins when some of our body's normal cells mutate, or change, thus creating cancerous cells. Sometimes this occurs naturally; sometimes it's caused by poisons in our air, water, or food.

Usually these cancerous cells are quickly recognized and destroyed by special **Natural Killer (NK) cells** in the immune system. But when the mutant cells aren't caught and they begin to multiply out of control, we develop cancer.

Even when the immune system works as it should, sometimes the invading bacteria or viruses are just too strong and the immune system needs outside help.

How Doctors Can Help

Doctors have many ways to help us fight disease. Doctors can give us **antibiotics**—medicines that help kill invaders, especially bacteria.

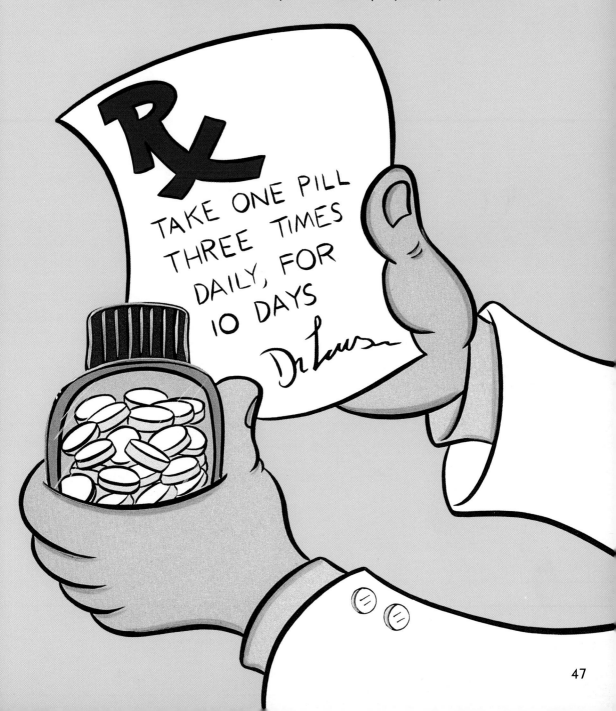

Immunization is another way doctors use their knowledge. Doctors can give us a **vaccine** with a substance that reminds the immune system of a particular disease.

This stimulates the immune system to make antibodies by making the white blood cells think there's a real invader when in fact there is only a decoy. Then when you are exposed to the real disease, your body already has lots of Memory T and B cells ready for that invader and can fight it off more easily.

Most children now get immunized against diseases, such as polio and measles, which used to kill many people. So many people were immunized against smallpox that now the disease no longer exists.

49

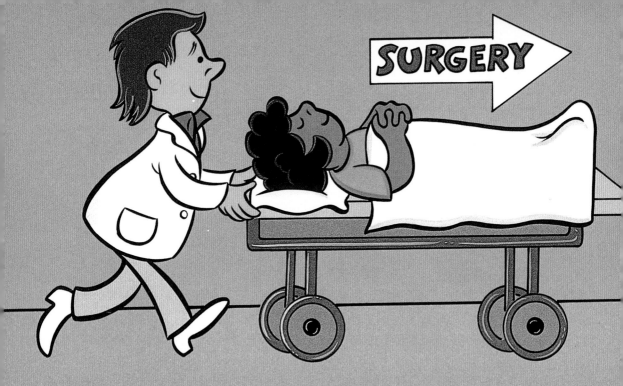

Doctors also have other tools to help our immune system fight infection or disease. Invaders or diseased cells can sometimes be removed by surgery or by draining the infected area. This helps the immune system by getting rid of most or all of the invaders.

When cancer cells multiply faster than the immune system can control them, doctors sometimes help by using **radiation therapy** or **chemotherapy** (powerful chemicals) to destroy them.

Doctors have been using antibiotics, vaccines, radiation, and chemotherapy for many years. As we learn more about exactly how the different parts of the immune system work, we are able to use that knowledge to fight disease. Much current research on disease focuses on how to protect and strengthen the immune system to help it fight better.

Scientists are now studying the chemical messengers in the immune system's communication network in attempts to prod it into action when it's weak or has failed.

And now that they understand how antibodies bind to invaders, scientists are creating 'magic bullets' by attaching strong poisons to the antibodies. The 'magic bullets' then go straight to the invaders, taking the poison directly to where it's needed.

Scientists can also remove some of the white blood cells that are trying to fight off an invader—

strengthen them and give them more ammunition—

and then put them back inside the body so they can better fight the invader.

Clues and Symptoms

Because the invaders are so small, you don't see them and you're not usually aware that these wars are going on inside your body. But there are clues that let you know your 'magic doctor' is busily at work. Often when you notice symptoms what's actually happening is that your body is working to fight an illness or injury. Let's look at some examples.

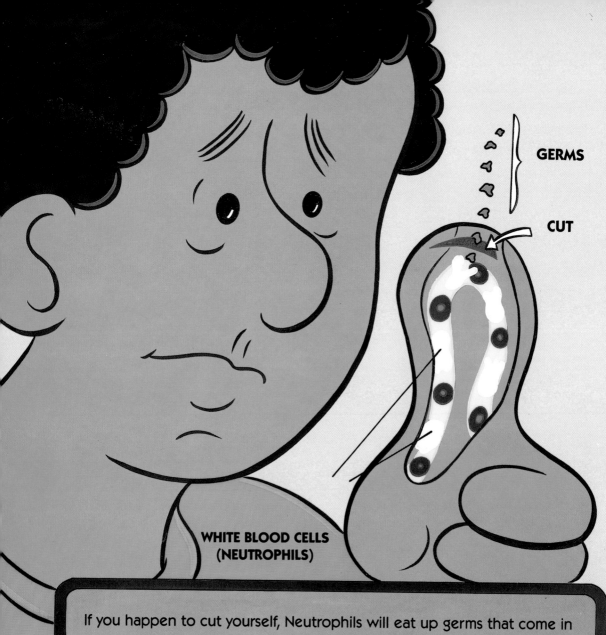

GERMS

CUT

WHITE BLOOD CELLS
(NEUTROPHILS)

If you happen to cut yourself, Neutrophils will eat up germs that come in through the cut. If too many germs get in and the cut gets infected, the redness and swelling you see comes from all the blood that rushes to the area, bringing more Neutrophils. The white pus you sometimes see around wounds or infections is actually just dead white cells left over after a battle. A scab will form over the cut and new skin cells will eventually grow back. It takes about a week for a cut to heal.

Some damage takes much longer to repair. When cigarette smoke damages your lungs, for example, it may take years without smoking for the lungs to heal.

When you get stung by a bee, the bee leaves a little poison under your skin. The bump is caused by all the white blood cells rush to the area to gobble up the poison.

LYMPH NODE

Swollen lymph nodes, such as you get with a sore throat, are a sign that there are lots of white blood cells inside the lymph nodes busily fighting off some invader.

WHITE BLOOD CELLS (NEUTROPHILS)

A doctor can tell if you have an infection by testing your blood. If there are many more white blood cells (especially Neutrophils) than normal, it means there is an infection somewhere in your body and your immune system is responding by releasing more white cells to fight the infection.

Fever is another tool the body has to fight infection. One of the signals the Macrophages send out when they spot an enemy can cause fever.

Fever seems to both slow down the invaders and speed up the white cells, making the invaders easier to overcome.

Fever may slow you down too—a signal to give your body the extra rest it needs in order to heal.

So instead of seeing all these symptoms as problems, you might see them as signs that your 'magic doctor' is hard at work—fixing whatever is wrong inside your body.

What You Can Do

There are lots of things you can do to help your body stay well, fight off disease, and heal from injuries. You know how people often tell you to eat good food and get plenty of rest and exercise? Well, now we know a lot more about why those things are important—and how they affect the immune system and the rest of the body.

WELLNESS PLAN

1. GOOD FOOD
2. REST
3. EXERCISE
4. LOW STRESS

Good food—filled with nutritious proteins, carbohydrates, fiber, vitamins, and minerals—

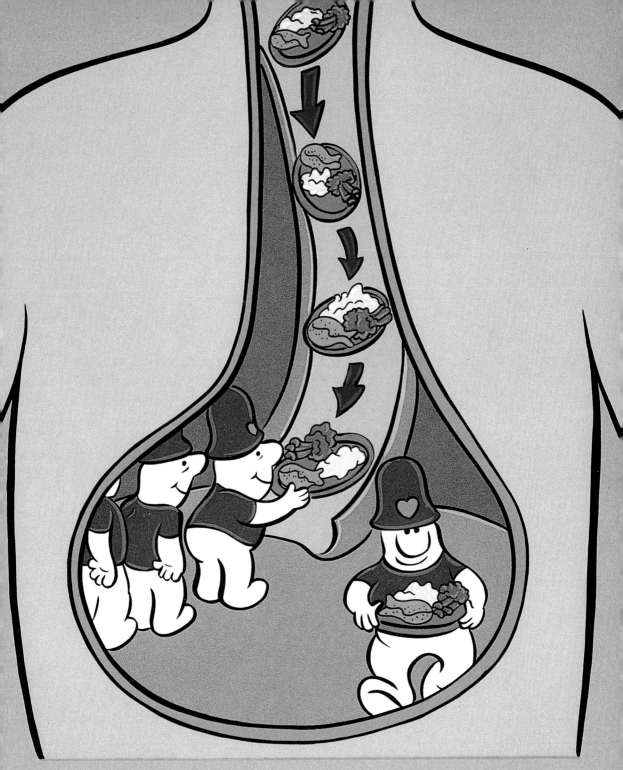

is needed by all the cells of your body, including the white blood cells, and
the new body cells that are constantly forming.

Exercise helps the body use the food we eat in a better way—and it can also help reduce stress.

Rest is also important—especially when you're sick.

And there are several other things to remember. Cleanliness can get rid of many germs before they are able to get inside your body and cause disease.

Avoiding another person's sneezes will also help keep out invading bacteria and viruses.

Smoking, alcohol, and other drugs can all harm your body—sometimes more than even the immune system can repair.

When your 'magic doctor' needs a friend,
remember that your real doctor is there too,
ready to lend a hand when your immune
system needs extra help.

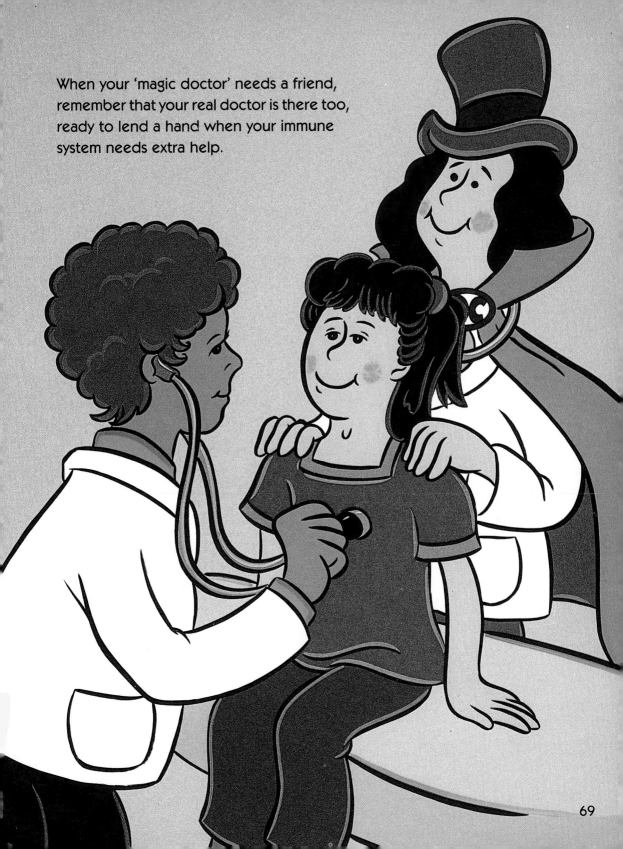

But remember that the most important help is the kind you can provide—by eating good food, getting plenty of rest and exercise, and by paying attention to what your body is telling you.

And, as you do these things, you can just imagine that your very own 'magic doctor' is already on the job, working to help you!

Glossary

AIDS (Acquired Immune Deficiency Syndrome). A disease caused by the HIV virus. The virus destroys the Helper T cells and cripples the effectiveness of the immune system.

Allergy An inappropriate reaction of the immune system to a particular substance (such as food, pollen, or dust) which is harmless to most people.

Antibiotic A medicine which can kill or decrease the growth of bacteria and other microorganisms.

Antibody A substance (protein) produced by B cells in response to a particular antigen. The antibody attaches to its antigen and initiates the destuction of the antigen.

Antigen A distinctive part of a microorganism that serves as a marker (fingerprint) for the immune system to recognize.

Autoimmune disease A disease in which the body attacks its own cells and molecules as if they were outside invaders.

B cell A white blood cell (lymphocyte), also found in the lymph nodes, that produces antibodies.

> **Memory B cell** A B cell that recognizes the antigens of microorganisms because of prior experience.

Bacteria (singular: **bacterium**) Microorganisms that can cause infection and disease.

Cancer A disease in which normal cells change and then begin to grow abnormally fast, forming tumors that can invade nearby normal areas and sometimes spread throughout the body.

Chemotherapy The use of powerful chemicals to treat disease.

Circulatory system The heart and the network of blood vessels (veins, capillaries, and arteries) that carry blood to every part of your body.

Fungus (plural: **fungi**) A microorganism that can cause infection and disease.

Germ A microorganism (bacteria, virus, or fungus) that can cause infection and disease.

Immune system The network of white blood cells and antibodies and other chemicals that the body produces to protect itself against infection and disease.

Immunity The ability of the immune system to recognize a microorganism as familiar because of previous infection or vaccination and thus rapidly make antibodies for that microorganism thereby preventing the microorganism from causing disease.

Immunization The process of making someone immune to a particular disease (see vaccine).

Immunodeficient Lacking natural immune defenses.

Lymph system A drainage network that begins in the tissues all over your body, filters through lymph nodes at certain points, and finally empties into a large vein and rejoins the circulatory system.

Lymph nodes Clumps of cells of the immune system that lie along the lymph channels.

Lymphocyte A type of white blood cell.

Macrophage A type of white blood cell (phagocyte) that engulfs and destoys invading microorganisms and foreign matter.

Microorganism A microscopic (very small) organism (such as bacteria, viruses, or fungi).

Natural Killer (NK) cell. A white cell (lymphocyte) that attacks cancer cells.

Neutrophil A white blood cell (phagocyte) that destroys invading microorganisms.

Phaghocyte A white blood cell that engulfs and destroys microorganisms anywhere in the body.

Plasma The straw-colored liquid part of the blood that carries the cells.

Platelet A component of blood that helps blood clotting.

Radiation therapy The use of radiation to treat disease.

Red blood cells The cells of the blood that carry oxygen.

T cell A white cell (lymphocyte) that develops in the thymus and becomes one of several types of T cells:

> **Helper T cell** A T cell that encourages production of antibodies.

> **Killer T cell** A T cell that can destroy other cells.

> **Memory T cell** A T cell that remembers the antigens of microorganisms it has previously encountered.

> **Suppressor T cell** A T cell that slows down the immune system after an invader has been defeated.

Thymus A gland which is important in the development of the immune system.

Vaccine A substance that stimulates an immune response to a particular microorganism for the purpose of creating Memory B and T cells to fight off that microorganism in the future.

Virus A microorganism that can invade body cells and cause infection. Viruses can only grow and reproduce by taking over body cells.

White blood cells The cells of the blood that fight disease.

Index

Order Form

Additional copies of **The Immune System: Your Magic Doctor** are available from Shire Press.

Cost: $15 (hardcover) or $10 (paper) plus $1.50 postage and handling per book. Bulk discounts available.

. . . .

_____ The Immune System: Your Magic Doctor (hardcover) ($15 each)

_____ The Immune System: Your Magic Doctor (paper) ($10 each)

Send book(s) to:

_____

_____

_____ zip _____

(Please enclose payment for books plus $1.50 postage and handling per book. California residents add sales tax.)

SHIRE PRESS   26873 Hester Creek Road, Los Gatos, CA 95030

. . . .

_____ The Immune System: Your Magic Doctor (hardcover) ($15 each)

_____ The Immune System: Your Magic Doctor (paper) ($10 each)

Send book(s) to:

_____

_____

_____ zip_____

(Please enclose payment for books plus $1.50 postage and handling per book. California residents add sales tax.)

SHIRE PRESS   26873 Hester Creek Road, Los Gatos, CA 95030